YANKEES LEGENDS ALPHABET

Words by Robin Feiner

A is for **A**lex Rodriguez. 'A-Rod' was an instant sensation after being traded to the Bronx Bombers in the winter of 2004, hitting 30 or more homers per year in his first seven seasons in New York. His defining moment came in the 2009 postseason when his legendary play helped carry the Yanks to their 27th pennant.

B is for **B**abe Ruth.
'The Babe', 'The Bambino'—
Ruth had many nicknames
because adoring Yanks fans
couldn't stop giving them to
him. After being traded by
the Red Sox (and leaving
them cursed), The Babe won
four World Series pennants
and became the undisputed
greatest player in Yankees'
history.

C is for **C**C Sabathia. The Yankees made a huge splash in 2008, signing Sabathia to the largest contract (at the time) for a pitcher in MLB history. And boy, CC didn't disappoint! He won 134 games and helped lead New York to a World Series title while wearing that legendary pinstriped uniform.

D is for **D**on Mattingly. A Yankee through and through, Mattingly played his entire 14-year career in the Bronx. His legendary manly moustache paired well with his overwhelming strength. Mattingly's greatest season came in 1985 when he led the American League in RBIs and won his only MVP award.

E is for Andy **E**ugene Pettitte. 219 wins. 2,020 strikeouts. 2,796 innings pitched. The statistics say it all: The man known only as 'Andy' was one of the greatest pitchers ever to lace 'em up for the New York Yankees. Over the course of his legendary career, Pettitte helped the Yanks capture five World Series titles.

F is for Whitey **F**ord.
The Yankees' all-time leader in wins and innings threw one heck of a mean fastball. He won double-digit games in 13 consecutive seasons in New York—and it certainly wasn't a coincidence he was named an All-Star in 10 of those seasons. Ford is a true New York legend.

G is for **G**eorge Steinbrenner. Love him or hate him for his meddling ways, 'The Boss' was responsible for much of New York's winning. As the longest-tenured owner in Yankees history, Steinbrenner helped bring home seven World Series pennants. So who cares if he occasionally (and irrationally) fired managers?

H is for **H**ideki Matsui. Beware the tremendous strength of the man known as 'Godzilla'. After coming over to the Yankees from Japan, Matsui became an instant fan favorite. He was cemented as a pinstriped legend in 2009 when he was named World Series MVP after batting in six RBIs in Game 6.

I is for **I**chiro Suzuki. While he only played three seasons in pinstripes, Ichiro certainly made his time in New York memorable. After being traded to the Yankees in 2012, he made an immediate impact, amassing 72 hits in 67 games and helping lead the team on a scorching run to the ALCS.

Jj

J is for Joe DiMaggio.
'Where have you gone,
Joe DiMaggio?' So beloved
was 'Joltin' Joe'—by Yankees
fans and the entire American
public—that Simon and
Garfunkel mentioned him
in their 1968 hit song, Mrs.
Robinson. Aside from The
Babe, DiMaggio might be
the most beloved legend
in Yankee history.

K is for Gary 'The Kraken' Sanchez. The Kraken has been slowly and steadily building a legendary résumé in New York. Through his first seven seasons, he's blasted 138 home runs and called several stellar games behind the plate for his pitchers.

L is for **L**ou Gehrig.
'The Iron Horse' was known
for his charming smile,
incredible durability, and
otherworldly hitting abilities.
Before his untimely death in
1941 from ALS, Gehrig set
several Yankees records.
Eighty years later, he still
holds the record for total
RBIs with a legendary 1,995.

M is for **M**ickey Mantle. The entire world loved 'The Mick', and The Mick loved them all back. His everyman personality helped Mantle become an all-time Yankees fan favorite. He helped the Bronx Bombers to seven World Series titles, all while crushing the most home runs (18) in World Series history.

N is for Derek 'Mr. **N**ovember' Jeter. "The great thing about being a Yankee is that you're always a Yankee." For some, the question of who's more legendary—Babe Ruth or Derek Jeter—is legitimate. Mr. November is New York's all-time leader in hits, stolen bases, and games played. Oh, and he won five World Series pennants.

O is for Reggie 'Mr. **O**ctober' Jackson. "REG-GIE! REG-GIE! REG-GIE!" On October 18th, 1977, Yankees fans couldn't stop chanting Mr. October's name. He'd hit three homers in Game 6 of the World Series, clinching another title for the Yanks. During five legendary seasons, Jackson's was the most powerful bat in the city.

P is for Jorge Posada. Posada played his entire 17-year career in pinstripes. His legendary presence behind the plate made him the ideal choice for any and every pitcher in the Yankees organization. He won four World Series titles, five Silver Slugger awards, and had his No. 20 jersey retired by the Yankees.

Qq

Q is for Mel Queen.
Only the most diehard of
Yanks fans will remember
Mr. Queen. He pitched four
on-and-off seasons for New
York in the 1940s, with his
best campaign in 1944. That
year, he pitched a dominant
3.31 ERA and finished fourth
on the team with six wins.

Rr

R is for **R**oger Maris. Maris was the meanest slugger in all of baseball. Rumor had it he could knock the ball right out of Yankee Stadium. In 1961, while playing for New York, he hit a then-MLB-record 61 home runs, each more crushing than the last. That record stood until 1998.

S is for Mariano 'Sandman' Rivera. At the end of the day, opponents never wanted to face the Sandman. And honestly, who in their right mind would want to face a pitcher who threw mid-90s cutting fastballs? Rivera is the greatest closer of all time and one of the best to ever don the Yankees' pinstripes.

T is for Joe **T**orre.
Torre took over as the
Yankees Manager in 1996.
His results that year? The best
record in baseball, a World
Series pennant, and status as
an instant legend in New York.
He won three more World
Series titles for the Yanks
and amassed 1,173 career
wins—the second-most in
Yankees' history.

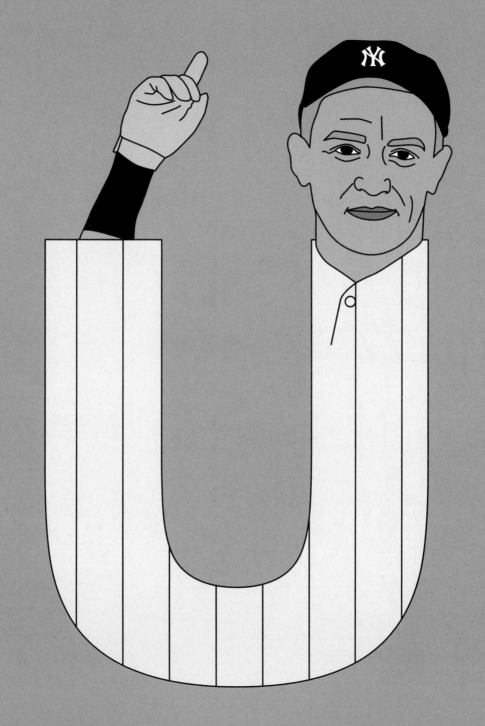

Uu

U is for **Urban Shocker.**
Shocker started and finished
his career in the Bronx,
establishing himself as a
legend by the time it was
all over. In 1927—his second-
to-last season—he compiled
a stunning 18-6 record and
a filthy 2.84 ERA, all while
leading the Yanks to their
second-ever World Series
pennant.

V is for **V**ic Raschi. Alongside Allie Reynolds and Eddie Lopat, Raschi helped form a 'Big Three' of pitchers for the Yankees. During a short and sweet legendary career in the Bronx, Vic notched 120 wins and helped the Yanks bring home six World Series titles.

W is for Roy **W**hite. Seeing as he was playing next to Thurman Munson and Reggie Jackson, it's no wonder Roy White was criminally underrated. But in die-hard Yankees circles, he is as revered as the next man. White was a crucial piece for the Yankees' Championship teams in '77 and '78.

X is for Mark 'Tex' Teixeira. Big Tex was a demolisher of baseballs. During a legendary career that saw him crush more than 400 homers, his greatest season came in 2009 in the Bronx Zoo. He had a blistering campaign that year, swatting 39 homers and helping the Yanks to a convincing World Series title.

Y is for **Y**ogi Berra.
Yogi epitomizes what legends are made of. He's the greatest catcher in Yankees and MLB history and a 10-time World Series champion. But most importantly, he played the game the right way: always with a smile on his glowing face.

Z is for Tom **Z**achary. Tom's name is famous in New York for many reasons. He gave up The Babe's 60th home run in 1927. Playing for the Yanks the following year, he helped them win the World Series. Amazingly, he pitched a 12-0 record for New York in 1929—an MLB record for the most wins without a loss.

The ever-expanding legendary library

EXPLORE THESE LEGENDARY ALPHABETS & MORE AT WWW.ALPHABETLEGENDS.COM

YANKEES LEGENDS ALPHABET
www.alphabetlegends.com

Published by Alphabet Legends Pty Ltd in 2022
Created by Beck Feiner
Copyright © Alphabet Legends Pty Ltd 2022

Printed and bound in China.

9780645200195

ALPHABET LEGENDS